W9-CZY-365

The Story of
Apple

Adam Sutherland

rosen publishing's
rosen central

New York

Published in 2012 by The Rosen Publishing Group, Inc.
29 East 21st Street, New York, NY 10010

Commissioning editor: Camilla Lloyd
Designer: Emma Randall
Picture researcher: Shelley Noronha

Library of Congress Cataloging-in-Publication Data

Sutherland, Adam.
 The story of Apple / Adam Sutherland.—1st ed.
    p. cm. — (The business of high tech)
 Includes bibliographical references and index.
 ISBN 978-1-4488-7040-0 (library binding)—ISBN 978-1-4488-7090-5 (pbk.)—ISBN 978-1-4488-7091-2 (6-pack)
1. Apple Computer, Inc.--History. 2. Computer industry--United States. I. Title.
HD9696.2.U64S88 2012
338.7'610040973--dc23
                                                                                                2011034301

Manufactured in the United States of America

CPSIA Compliance Information: Batch #W12YA: For further information, contact Rosen Publishing, New York, New York, at 1-800-237-9932.

Picture Acknowledgments: The author and publisher would like to thank the following for allowing their pictures to be reproduced in this publication: Cover and 16: Getty Images; throughout background: RedShineStudio/Istockphoto; pp. 1, 2 100 words/Shutterstock; pp. 5, 11, 25, Getty Images; pp. 6–7, 20 Bloomberg via Getty Images; pp. 10 Roger Ressmeyer/Corbis; 8 SSPL via Getty Images; 12–13 Sipa Press/Rex Features; 15 AFP Getty Images; 18–19 Imaginechina/Corbis; 21 Xinhua/Photoshot; 22 Yi Lu/Corbis; 23 Lai Xiangdong/Xinhua Press/Corbis; 24 Wirelmage/Getty; 28-29 Bloomberg via Getty Images; 30–31 Ivan Stevanovic/Istockphoto; 32–33 Chris Hutchison/Istockphoto; 34-35 Lai Xiangdong/Xinhua Press/Corbis; 36 Wirelmage/Getty; 37 Getty Images; 38-39, 41, 42-43 Getty Images; 44 Ivan Stevanovic/Istockphoto; 48 Chris Hutchison/Istockphoto.

Every attempt has been made to clear copyright for this edition. Should there be any inadvertent omission, please apply to the publisher for rectification.

Contents

An Apple in Every Home

Apple is flying high. The company that invented the personal computer has successfully branched out into music and telecommunications. Today there are 50 million iPhone and iPod users, over 500 million active iTunes users worldwide, and sales of the iPad, Apple's flat-screen "tablet" PC, reached 7 million by the end of 2010, with 57 million sales per year estimated by 2015.

With revenues of $26.7 billion in 2010, Apple is now the largest mobile-device company in the world, and its shares are worth roughly 43 times their level of ten years ago.

The iTunes Store has even overtaken America's largest supermarket chain Wal-Mart to become the largest retailer of music in the USA.

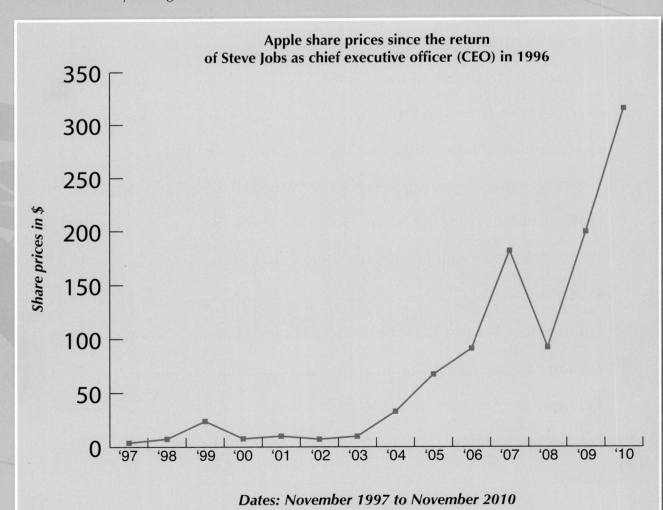

Apple share prices since the return of Steve Jobs as chief executive officer (CEO) in 1996

Dates: November 1997 to November 2010

An Apple in Every Home

Steve Jobs launches the iPod Touch in 2009.

But Apple's story, similar to the story of one of its founders, Steve Jobs, is full of downs as well as ups. Apple's skill has always been innovation. It created the world's first truly personal computer, the Apple II, in 1977 and made groundbreaking machines that the industry loved, and that consumers wanted to have in their homes. But somewhere along the line the focus got lost, and the company started to fall behind more business-oriented companies like IBM and Microsoft in the race to put computers on every office desk in the world.

Steve Jobs was forced out of Apple, and he ended up turning Pixar (an animation company) into the most successful and well-respected computer animation studio in the world. Steve never lost his love for Apple, however, and he eventually returned to the company in 1996 to start an incredible phase of growth and success that continues to this day.

In the following pages, you will read about the founding of Apple, the machines it has produced, and the decisions it has made — good and bad — that have created the Apple that we all know today. Along the way, you'll discover more about the years of development that go into creating great products, and the inspired business planning that has helped Apple expand into new markets, stay one step ahead of the competition and, most importantly, stay on top.

> ❝ I was worth over a million dollars when I was 23, and over ten million dollars when I was 24, and over a hundred million dollars when I was 25, and it wasn't that important because I never did it for the money. ❞
>
> **Steve Jobs**

CHAPTER 2

The Origins of Apple

Apple was founded in April 1976 by Steve Jobs and Steve Wozniak. The pair met in 1969 when Jobs was still in high school. Wozniak — known as "Woz" — was working at computer company Hewlett-Packard and had a reputation as the local electronics whiz kid. "He was the first person I met who knew more electronics than I did," Jobs remembers.

In 1960s Silicon Valley, it was cool to be into electronics, and the two men became regulars at a local computer hobbyists' group called the Homebrew Computer Club. Woz would pick up ideas at meetings and then go home and work on them so that he could impress his fellow "techies" at the next gathering. He enjoyed doing things better, with fewer parts and more elegant engineering, than anyone believed possible. If Woz had the know-how, Jobs had the get-up-and-go. When he had an objective, nothing stood in his way of reaching it.

In 1975, the world's first "personal computer," the Altair, was launched. It came in kit form and, once constructed, just lit up a line of bulbs when you entered the correct — and complicated — binary codes. It was an electronic breakthrough, and Jobs started planning how they could profit from this new field. Jobs and Wozniak formed a company and named it Apple Computer — partly because of Jobs's love of pop music (the Beatles' record label was also called Apple), and partly because "Apple" would come before "Atari" — Jobs's former employer — in the phone book.

Woz started building circuit boards that hobbyists could then load up with components to create their own basic computer. The plan was to build these boards for $25 each, and sell them for $50. Instead, they were persuaded by local computer store owner Paul Terrell that they would do better business if they produced and sold ready-stocked boards. These boards — Apple's first product — were called Apple I. Terrell's Byte Shop ordered 50 at $500 each — a first order worth $25,000. Apple was on its way!

Steve Jobs launches the iPad in 2010 in the foreground with a picture of him and cofounder Steve Wozniak in the background.

This picture shows Steve Wozniak in 1984. Woz left Apple in 1987, but he remains a shareholder in the company. In September 2000, he was inducted into the National Inventors Hall of Fame.

Brains Behind the Brand

Steve Wozniak – Cofounder of Apple
Computer engineer Steve Wozniak — known as "Woz" — is often credited as the person who started the personal computer revolution. His Apple II design, introduced in 1977, brought computers onto the desks of ordinary people. Sold as a finished computer, rather than as a kit, it was accessible to the mass market rather than just to hobbyists and fellow engineers.

A plane crash in 1981 left Woz with significant memory loss, and although he returned to work in 1983, he was no longer active in new product development.

> *Steve Jobs didn't really set the direction of my Apple I and Apple II designs, but he did the more important part of turning them into a product that would change the world.*
> **Steve Wozniak**

Building the Apple Brand

By the end of 1976, Apple had sold 150 Apple Is, representing nearly $100,000 in revenue. Woz was making nearly as much money from Apple as he was from his day job at Hewlett-Packard, but wasn't ready to commit himself to Apple full time.

However, he was committed to improving on his own Apple I design. The Apple I was a fully assembled circuit board containing more than 60 chips. However, to turn it into a working computer, users still had to add a case, a power supply, a keyboard, and even a monitor. Woz soon followed the Apple I with the Apple II, single-handedly designing all its hardware and software — an extraordinary feat for the time. And what's more, he did it all while working at his day job at Hewlett-Packard!

The Apple II came as a finished product, rather than as a kit, with a built-in monitor, keyboard, sound and high-resolution graphics. Presented to the public in 1977 at the first major computer trade show in California, the West Coast Computer Faire, it was the first computer designed for the mass market, not just for engineers and computer "nerds."

Around the same time, Steve Jobs saw an ad campaign for electronics company Intel. Rather than focus on the science, the ad used poker chips, hamburgers and racing cars to explain how great Intel was. Jobs tracked down the man who dreamed up the ad, Regis McKenna, and refused to leave his office until he took on Apple as a client!

McKenna and Jobs both agreed that the key to the company's growth was in reaching beyond the hobbyist market, and selling the idea that "computers are for everyone." It's an idea that Apple still uses successfully to this day.

◄ The revolutionary Apple II was the first computer to be sold as a finished product.

The Apple computer store in Tokyo, Japan, shows the familiar Apple logo.

Brains Behind the Brand

Susan Kare – Graphic artist at Apple

Susan joined Apple in 1982 and originally worked in the Macintosh software team, designing fonts and user interface graphics — the icons that appear on your computer screen depicting everything from the hard disk to the wastebasket. Her most recognizable works from her time with Apple are the Chicago typeface (used on the first four generations of the iPod), the Geneva typeface, and the Happy Mac symbol (the smiling computer that welcomed Mac users when they started their machines).

Business Matters

Branding — All the qualities and features of a product, including its name and its appearance, are presented to the customer as a brand. To be successful, all brands — from Apple to McDonald's to Nike — need to be distinctive (stand out in some way from competitors), consistent (always provide the same level of quality, and therefore be seen as reliable), recognizable (through a logo or "look" of a product) and attractive. Everyone recognizes Apple's half-eaten apple logo!

Fallout at the Top

Helped by several innovative software programs, including the first accounting spreadsheet Visicalc, the Apple II became a huge seller, and Apple became the world's number one personal computer company. By 1980 it had grown to 1,000 employees and had manufacturing plants as far apart as California, Ireland and Singapore.

The Lisa featured a detachable keyboard, mouse and graphical user interface. Its high price meant it was not a market success.

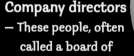

Company directors — These people, often called a board of directors, oversee the activities of a company. A board's role is determined by the powers and responsibilities granted to it by a company's own rules and regulations. These rules usually cover the number of members on the board, how they are chosen, and how often they meet. The board usually chooses one of its members to be the chairman. Typical duties of a board include: setting the rules that run the organization; selecting, appointing, supporting and reviewing the performance of the CEO; approving annual budgets; and reporting to shareholders on the company's performance.

In December of that same year, Apple shares went on sale on the New York Stock Exchange in a process called an IPO (which means "initial public offering"). The 4.6 million shares were sold within one hour, in the most successful IPO since the Ford Motor Company's in 1956. Overnight, Steve Jobs was worth $217.5 million, making him one of the USA's richest men.

Steve's passion and drive for excellence meant that he worked his employees hard. He earned $250,000 per year in salary, but insisted that each of his engineers earn no more than $30,000 — they were the lowest-paid engineers at Apple — plus he expected his team to work 80-90 hours per week. Steve was trying to ensure that his engineers really wanted to work for Apple rather than to make a lot of money. Most still loved him for his genius and desperately wanted to work on Steve's projects.

Brains Behind the Brand

Mike Markkula – Former CEO of Apple

Steve Jobs convinced Mike of the huge potential market for the Apple II and personal computers in general.

Mike provided important managerial experience and support for the new company, along with a $250,000 investment, and he became a one-third owner of Apple, and employee number three. Mike brought order and structure to the young company, hiring Apple's first president, Michael Scott, and serving as chairman himself from 1985 until 1997. Steve Wozniak credits Mike — even more than his own innovative computer designs — for the long-term success of Apple.

Mike Markkula with the first Apple II computer and its carrying case in 1977.

However, Steve went on to make several expensive mistakes. New computers like the Apple III, and the high-powered business machine the Lisa both flopped, and the first Macintosh, which was meant to save the company, could only generate 10 percent of the sales that Steve had predicted. Customers complained about the lack of software programs, the shortage of memory, and the small screen. Steve was getting wrapped up in design and forgetting to give the customers the functions that they wanted.

Apple sales stalled, the company announced a financial loss, and share prices fell as a result. The Apple board of directors acted quickly, removing Steve from his position as chairman, and putting John Sculley (the former head of Pepsi) in his place. Steve resigned from the company he founded on May 28, 1985.

Steve Returns to Apple

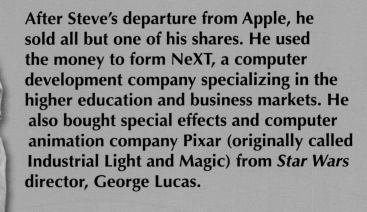

After Steve's departure from Apple, he sold all but one of his shares. He used the money to form NeXT, a computer development company specializing in the higher education and business markets. He also bought special effects and computer animation company Pixar (originally called Industrial Light and Magic) from *Star Wars* director, George Lucas.

Through NeXT, Steve was learning valuable lessons about the importance of balancing hardware (a computer's outer look and feel) and software (what it actually does). At the same time, he was turning Pixar from a company that lost $1 million per month into Hollywood's most respected and successful computer animation studio. Steve's biggest success came when Pixar agreed to a distribution deal with Disney, and the first film they co-produced was the hugely successful *Toy Story*.

Meanwhile, Apple was struggling. Computers from its main competitor IBM, powered by Windows software produced by Microsoft, were used in

Gil Amelio, CEO of Apple in 1996.

Business Matters

Mergers and acquisitions — This phrase refers to the aspect of company strategy and finance that deals with the buying, selling and combining of different companies. This strategy can help a company grow rapidly within its market without having to create another separate company. An acquisition is the purchase of one company by another company, as when Apple bought NeXT. A merger is when two companies combine to form a third, new company.

> " Getting fired from Apple was the best thing that could have ever happened to me. The heaviness of being successful was replaced by the lightness of being a beginner again... It freed me to enter one of the most creative periods of my life. "
>
> **Steve Jobs**

virtually all businesses around the world. Steve's successor John Sculley had been unable to improve Apple's fortunes. While he was chairman, Apple's market share (the percentage of computers it sold compared to every other company) fell from 20 percent to just 8 percent. Apple directors started to look around for someone to buy the company. Revenues were so low that no one was interested!

Instead, Apple hired a new chairman, Gil Amelio, former president and CEO of technology company National Semiconductor. One of the first calls Gil received was from Steve Jobs. Steve told Gil that as the company's cofounder, he was the only person who could put Apple back on track.

Eventually, Steve got his wish. In 1996, Apple executives were searching for a new operating system to power their next wave of computers, and Steve persuaded Gil to buy NeXT. In exchange for $377.5 million and 1.5 million Apple shares, Gil acquired all Steve's 300 staff and his NeXTSTEP software system. The financial figures for 1997 showed that Apple sales had fallen to $7 billion, and losses were over $1 billion. The board asked Gil to step down and appointed Steve Jobs as CEO!

The first Toy Story *film was released in 1995.*

Riding the Internet Wave

Steve was back at the company he loved, but there was no time to celebrate. Apple was in trouble, and he needed to act quickly. One of Steve's first calls was to Bill Gates, the owner of Microsoft. The pair quickly struck a deal.

In exchange for investing $150 million in Apple, Microsoft would produce and sell Microsoft Office products for the Macintosh. Apple would also install Microsoft's Internet Explorer Web browser on all Macs sold. Apple fans booed the announcement at the MacWorld exhibition in Boston in 1997, but Steve knew that without market leader Microsoft's support, Apple was in real danger of becoming irrelevant and outdated.

Steve was probably the only man who could bring order to the chaotic corporate culture that he had created when he formed Apple. He cut back on company spending — axing 70 percent of new products in development, putting a stop to expensive business-class travel for employees — and replaced the whole board of directors who had employed him!

By January 1998, Apple was again making a profit — even though sales had fallen slightly to $5.9 billion — and by January 2000 the company's market value had risen from $2 billion to over $16 billion.

The board granted Steve $870 million worth of Apple stock for his efforts, as well as his own Gulfstream V corporate jet.

But what was next? Steve was convinced that he needed to catch the start of the Internet wave. If he could combine the freedom of the Internet with the simplicity and great design of the Mac, he was sure it would be a winning combination. The result was the iMac, a combined monitor and hard drive with funky colored plastic side panels that sold for $1,300 and came loaded with everything you needed to go online. "Plug and play" was the concept: open the box, plug it in, and get surfing! The idea was revolutionary — and Apple sold two million iMacs in just over a year.

Another of Apple's innovations was the iBook, an iMac-inspired laptop, which offered something called "Airport" — the ability to connect wirelessly to the Internet. Other companies were offering this, but Apple made the most noise about it, and it worked. Apple was back on top.

Steve Jobs launches the iBook in 1999.

The iMac came in a variety of colors.

Brains Behind the Brand

Steve Jobs – Former Chairman and CEO of Apple

Steve Jobs was one of the world's most well-known and well-respected businessmen. Steve cofounded Apple in 1976, and 20 years later returned to turn around its fortunes. As Apple's CEO, it was Steve's job to develop company strategy and make sure everyone within Apple followed it.

A CEO's main roles are to facilitate business outside of the company and to guide employees toward clearly defined objectives. For example, Steve wanted to expand Apple beyond a computer company and make it an entertainment company. He gave new directions to research departments to focus on music, and then telecommunications, and hired new specialized employees where necessary to get the job done.

> *Innovation distinguishes between a leader and a follower.*
>
> ***Steve Jobs***

Apple Explores Music

Steve wanted to make Apple products a part of people's everyday lives. Then they would never turn their backs on the company again. His next focus was music. Apple scouts had discovered a software program called SoundJam MP, owned by a small company called Casady and Greene (C&G), which allowed people to play MP3 files (digital music files).

Apple made C&G an offer: Sell us the rights to SoundJam, or we'll develop a competitive product and put you out of business. C&G had little choice but to agree. It also lost SoundJam's original developer Jeff Robbin to Apple's in-house team. By January 2001, Apple was able to announce the launch of "iTunes" — a simple, free download that meant Macintosh users could copy tracks from a CD onto their computer and play them digitally.

Users could also download the files onto portable MP3 players, although sales of these devices at the time were very low. Steve decided this was because the products were badly designed, and he saw another opportunity for Apple to capture a market. He hired hardware developer Tony Fadell, who based his designs on an existing product called PortalPlayer.

◄ *Apple has cool and very distinctive advertising.*

> **"** Without the iPod, the digital music age would have been defined by files and folders instead of songs and albums. Though the medium of music has changed, the iPod experience has kept the spirit of what it means to be a music lover alive. **"**
>
> ### John Mayer, singer and songwriter

Apple's prototype was shrunk down, and its usability improved. Designer Jonathan Ive oversaw the look of the new product, and on October 23, 2001, Apple introduced its first iPod, with enough storage for 1,000 songs.

Sales gradually grew, with 140,000 sold between July and September 2002, and 200,000 sold between October and Christmas. The iPod became the company's most successful product. The final part of the plan was the iTunes Music Store, announced in April 2003, which allows users to purchase and download music online. Apple's secure downloading process and payment system won over the record companies' concerns about the increased threat of piracy and illegal downloading.

The iTunes Store opened its doors with a library of 200,000 songs, each available for 99 cents. Within a year, Apple had taken over 70 percent of the legal music download business, selling 85 million songs, and the iTunes Music Store was named *Fortune* magazine's Product of the Year.

Brains Behind The Brand

Tony Fadell – Former senior vice president of the iPod Division
A computer engineering graduate from the University of Michigan, Tony joined Apple as the first member of its iPod hardware engineering team in 2001, and is credited as the man responsible for bringing the world's most successful digital music player to market.

Tony was promoted to vice president of iPod engineering in 2004, and became senior vice president of the iPod Division in April 2006, before leaving Apple in 2008.

CHAPTER 8
The Invention of the iPhone

An ad for the iPhone in China.

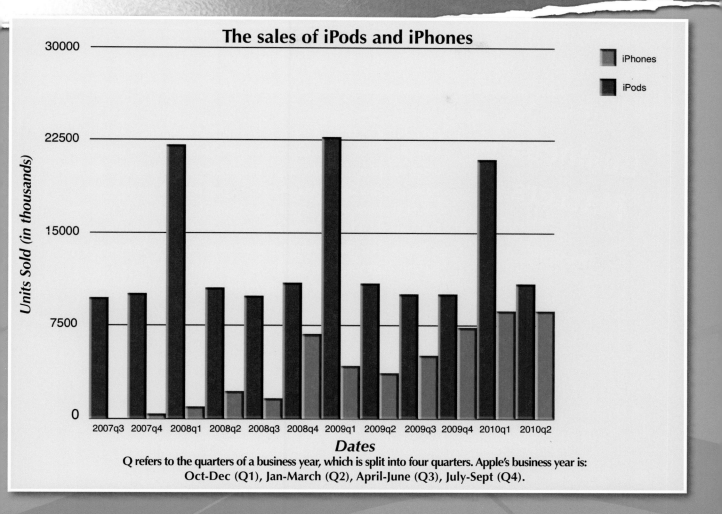

The sales of iPods and iPhones

Units Sold (in thousands)

- iPhones
- iPods

30000
22500
15000
7500
0

2007q3 2007q4 2008q1 2008q2 2008q3 2008q4 2009q1 2009q2 2009q3 2009q4 2010q1 2010q2

Dates

Q refers to the quarters of a business year, which is split into four quarters. Apple's business year is:
Oct-Dec (Q1), Jan-March (Q2), April-June (Q3), July-Sept (Q4).

This graph shows the sales of iPods and iPhones over a three-year period. Apple sold 22,727,000 iPods in the first quarter of 2009.

Part of the secret to any business's continued success is looking ahead to how a market might change and how its products can stay relevant. In 2002, even before Apple released the first iPod, Steve Jobs began thinking about developing a phone. At the time, millions of people were carrying separate phones, BlackBerrys for e-mail, and MP3 players, and Steve was sure that a single device combining all three would be extremely popular.

Business Matters

Advertising — This is a form of communication intended to persuade an audience (viewers, readers or listeners) to purchase or take some action regarding products, ideas, or services. Advertising includes the name of a product or service and how that product or service could benefit the consumer, in order to persuade the consumer to purchase that particular brand. These messages are viewed via various media — TV, print, etc. Advertising can also communicate an idea to a large number of people in an attempt to convince them to take a certain action, for example, to vote in an election.

By the summer of 2004, 3G phones (which allowed users to surf the Internet and download data at high speed) were becoming more popular, Wi-Fi phones were on the horizon, and rivals to the iTunes Music Store were appearing. At the time, the iPod accounted for 16 percent of Apple revenues, and Steve saw a danger that if another company came up with this device before Apple, the iPod's dominance as a music player would be threatened.

Steve approached handset manufacturer Motorola, and together they developed the ROKR phone, launched in September 2005. Unfortunately, the phone was a flop — it looked boring, was hard to use, and could only hold 100 songs.

The answer, Steve realized, was for Apple to design its own phone. There were numerous challenges to overcome — from developing revolutionary touch-screen technology, to rewriting a complete operating system that would make the phone work, to ensuring that the phone was safe and didn't emit dangerous levels of radiation.

After an estimated $150 million was spent on development, the iPhone went on sale on June, 29 2007. In the US, Steve struck a unique deal with mobile carrier AT&T:

in return for five years' exclusivity with AT&T, 10 percent of iPhone sales in AT&T stores, and a small percentage of iTunes revenue, Apple received $10 per month from every iPhone customer's AT&T bill. Most importantly, it retained complete control over design, manufacturing and marketing of the phone.

The iPhone was everything Steve wanted it to be, and it was a huge success. Its looks, ease of use, and great range of functions helped it sell three million handsets in the first six months, and six million in the first year. With an estimated $80 profit on every $399 phone sold, it also became Apple's most profitable product.

There's an App for That!

The iPhone became a must-have device. But must-have devices can quickly disappear if consumers find something more interesting, or more fun, to move on to. What really kept the iPhone on top was the launch of the App Store in July 2008.

This is the popular Angry Birds game being played on an iPad.

The App Store was the direct result of Apple inviting outside software developers to create applications for the iPod Touch, iPhone and most recently the iPad. The Software Development Kit (SDK) for the iPhone was announced in March 2008, and it allowed any developer to create applications and distribute them through the App Store on iTunes.

All applications have to pass Apple's approval process for basic reliability and suitability, and they are rated based on their content regarding what age group they are suitable for. The four ratings are 4+, 7+, 12+ and 17+. Depending on the application, some are given away free, and others cost anywhere from $.99 to $8.00 and above. Apple takes 30 percent of any revenues generated, and passes 70 percent on to the app's developer.

Business Matters

Profit and loss — A profit and loss statement is a company's financial report that indicates how the revenue (money received from the sale of products and services before expenses are taken out, also known as the "top line") is transformed into the net income (the result after all revenues and expenses have been taken out, also known as the "bottom line"). The revenues for a specific period are shown, and the costs and expenses charged against those revenues. The purpose of the profit and loss statement is to show company managers and investors whether the company made or lost money during the period being reported.

The App Store was an instant success. It took Apple over three years to hit two billion song downloads from iTunes, but it took less than one and a half years to hit two billion app downloads! On the day of the launch, 500 apps were available. Ten million downloads were made during the first weekend alone, and the numbers continued at a rate of half a million downloads a day, generating $1 million per day in revenues. As of October 20, 2010, the number of apps in the store had grown to over 300,000!

Brains Behind the Brand

Eddy Cue – Vice president for Internet Services

Eddy gradually became one of Steve Jobs's most trusted deputies. Eddy was given the job of creating the iTunes Store and then, alongside Steve, his role grew to negotiating with record labels and Hollywood film studios for content to fill it!

iTunes was quickly clocking up millions of downloads per week, and Eddy's next project was the App Store. He has turned it into the best-used app service on the Internet, a long way ahead of Google, Microsoft and Research In Motion, which produces the BlackBerry. Eddy's next big project is tackling the eBook market and creating a successful iBook Store for the iPad.

Not surprisingly, this had made a significant contribution to Apple's annual revenues. In June 2010, Steve Jobs announced that there had been 5 billion app downloads in two years, with Apple earning around $410 million from its 30 percent cut of sales.

WeatherBug · AIM · BeatMaker · Expenses

Remote · Loopt · Express · Cro-Mag

Mandarin · PAC-MAN · ForeFlight · GuitarToolkit

Lucky 7 Slots · AOL Radio · Scrabble · Currency

Phone · Mail · Safari

TETRIS

32

AccuFuel
$0.99 · A powerful
tool to monitor
your vehicle's
fuel efficiency.

OmniFocus
$19.99 · Bring task
management to
your fingertips.

Free · Access
headline
and ph
this trust

Eye-catching graphics advertise the hundreds of apps available from the App Store.

CHAPTER 10
Apple Takes on Publishing

For any company that thrives on growth, it is vitally important to keep innovating and moving forward. Apple's next decision was to start to overhaul its personal computer division. By combining the look and feel of the iPhone into a large (9.5 in x 7.3 in [243 mm x 190 mm]) tablet PC with a touch screen, it was able to offer the most popular functions that computer users wanted — e-mail, gaming, music, access to the Internet — in a device that it knew users would love.

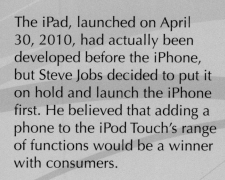

Business Matters

Diversification — Companies often decide to offer new products or services, like the iPhone and the App Store, because it reduces the risk of their other products becoming too limited or uninteresting. By adding new products to its line, Apple gives consumers more reasons to buy Apple products. When companies offer a completely different product or service, like supermarkets offering car or house insurance, this is called "brand stretching".

The iPad, launched on April 30, 2010, had actually been developed before the iPhone, but Steve Jobs decided to put it on hold and launch the iPhone first. He believed that adding a phone to the iPod Touch's range of functions would be a winner with consumers.

Weighing just 1.5 pounds (680 grams) with a 9.7-in (246-mm) diagonal LCD touchscreen, the iPad sits between the smaller iPhone and the laptop. It is aimed at the games, movie and music market, and at the book, magazine and newspaper market. This has sent shock waves through the publishing industry.

By the launch date, Apple had built an iBookstore as part of

People can use the iPad to navigate their route and find out where they are going.

> " [The] iPad is... a stunningly exciting object, one that you will want now and one that will not be matched this year by any company. "
>
> ***Stephen Fry, TV presenter and technology enthusiast***

iTunes (at the time of going to press, this is currently only available in the USA) and had agreements with major US publishers, including Penguin, Macmillan, HarperCollins and Simon & Schuster, to publish books for the iPad. Several magazines and newspapers, including *GQ*, *Vanity Fair*, *Wired* and the *New York Times,* have also released iPad versions.

It's too early to tell whether the iPad will cause the death or the rebirth of publishing, but it has already helped increase publishers' sales. Because Apple only takes a 30 percent cut from eBook sales through iTunes, the other great online retailer Amazon has been forced to reduce its own cut of book sales from 50 percent down to 30 percent to stay competitive. The iPad has also proved a huge success with consumers. By selling 7.5 million units in its first five months, it became the fastest-selling consumer electronics device in history — faster than the iPhone and even the DVD player! By the summer of 2011, Apple had sold 29 million iPads.

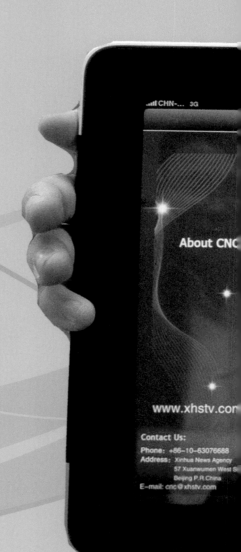

You can watch and read the news on an iPad.

CHAPTER 11

What Makes Apple Products "Must-haves"?

If there is one secret ingredient, one USP (unique selling proposition or point) behind Apple's success, it is the understanding of the importance of good design. From the Apple I in 1976 right up to the iPad in 2010, each and every one of Apple's products has been built to look great and to stand apart as iconic timeless designs. The hope is that consumers will love to look at them, just as much as they love to use them.

Apple is fortunate to have an award-winning designer, Jonathan Ive as its head of Industrial Design. According to Jonathan, Apple was just as lucky to have a chairman like Steve Jobs, who was "an exceptional designer" and shared Jonathan's love of excellent design.

Together, Jonathan and Steve were held responsible for Apple's ability to delight and dazzle consumers with their famous products, from the brightly colored iMac that changed people's perceptions of what a PC should look like, to the tiny iPod Nano and iPod Shuffle.

So how can Apple create mass-produced products that look like they were made by hand? In a 1996 interview, Steve said, "Design is a funny word. Some people think design means how [a product] looks. But, of course, if you dig deeper, it's really how [a product] works. To design something really well, you have to 'get it.'"

Jonathan agrees. He credits his success down to limiting the number of projects he works on, caring deeply about the products he designs, and focusing only on what's important and what will make a product stand out as different.

For his outstanding design work, Jonathan was named "the most influential person in British culture" for 2004, beating Harry Potter author JK Rowling!

To create a plastic shell for the first iMac, and to make it look exciting rather than cheap, Jonathan and his team spent time in a candy factory studying how jelly beans were made! They then spent months in Asia with manufacturers, producing case after case until they found a way to make millions every year to the same high standards. They even requested that the internal electronics be redesigned so that they look nicer through the see-through casing. With dedication like that, it's not hard to see why Apple is regarded as the most design-oriented company in the world.

> *From early on, we wanted a product that would seem so natural and so inevitable and so simple, you almost wouldn't think of it as having been designed.*
>
> **Jonathan Ive, on the iPod**

The Nano has become one of Apple's most popular products.

Brains Behind the Brand

Jonathan Ive – Senior vice President for Industrial Design
Jonathan was hired by Apple in 1992. When Steve Jobs returned to Apple and closed down production on all but four of Apple's 60 products, he started to search for a design superstar to rejuvenate Apple's product line. Jonathan expected to lose his job. Instead, Steve realized the genius he was looking for was right under his nose, and he put Jonathan in charge!

The pair's success started with the first iMac and now includes the iPod, iPhone, iPad, MacBook Air and many more products.

CHAPTER 12

What Does the Future Hold for Apple?

Apple has built a fantastic reputation for innovation, style and fun. It seems to guess what consumers want, even before we know we want it!

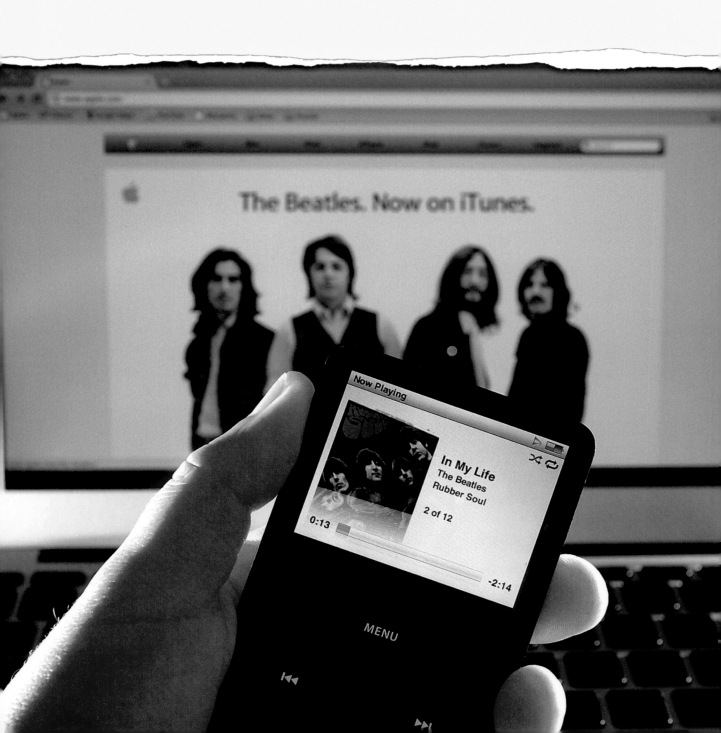

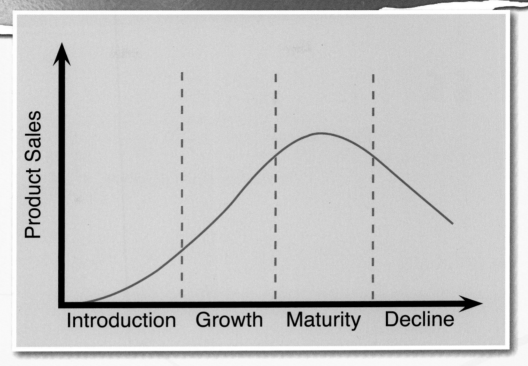

↑ *The graph above shows the natural growth and decline cycle for any product, for example, the iMac, iPod and iPhone. It clearly shows the reason why Apple needs to keep innovating and introducing great new products!*

Although no one apart from the most trusted employees really know what Apple's plans are for the next ten years, it's fair to assume the company will continue to focus on entertainment — specifically, music, movies, games and television. And here's the evidence.

First, Apple's hold on the handheld gaming market was up 53.2 percent in 2010 from the previous year, with 43.8 percent of gamers playing on the iPhone and iPod Touch rather than the Nintendo DS and Sony PSP. The much-anticipated iPad 2 launched in 2011 and suggests a move by Apple to strengthen its hold on this market.

← *The Beatles' albums finally became available on iTunes in 2010.*

> " The resurrection of Apple is the most astounding story that's happened in business in at least a decade. You might be able to go further and say a half-century. It's on par with [the inventions of] Thomas Edison and Alexander Graham Bell in terms of its total impact. "
>
> **Technology expert Roger Kay**

Second, Apple is trying various tactics to give its music sales a boost. iTunes will soon be offering 90-second instead of 30-second sample clips of songs. Plus amazing deals like offering the Beatles' back catalogue for the first time on iTunes generates huge amounts of traffic. Over two million singles, and 450,000 albums, were downloaded in the first seven days!

Third, Apple launched a Mac App Store in early 2011, to boost revenues in the desktop computer market. And, last but not least, Apple has plans to take over your living room!

The original Apple TV was launched in 2007; the second-generation device came out just before the holidays in 2010. The square-shaped box allows users to rent standard and HD films through iTunes and play them on your TV; play your iTunes library through your TV speakers; listen to podcasts and visit Web sites like YouTube and Flickr; and stream TV shows over the Internet. Apple TV is a little ahead of its time, and it is unlikely to become the next iPod or iPhone overnight, but it shows clearly where Apple is looking — to the future of entertainment! And who would bet on Apple not finding another world-changing product in the next few years?

Steve Jobs launches Apple TV in 2010.

To create a new product, it is helpful to put together a product development brief like the one below. This is a sample brief for the Space Hopper app. The SWOT analysis on the opposite page can help you to think about the strengths, weaknesses, opportunities and threats of your product. This can let you see how feasible and practical your idea is before you think of investing in it.

Product Development Brief

Name of application : Space Hopper

Design of logo

The product explained (use 25 words or less) : The fun never stops! Shake your phone to bounce. Keep bouncing over bigger and bigger obstacles to win points. Great lo-tech entertainment.

Target age of users : 5-100

What does the product do? Space Hopper is a simple platform game that allows iPhone owners to use the motion-sensor on their phone to activate the game's "bounces." It is simple and addictive.

Are there any similar products already available? Lots — games like Angry Birds and Doodle Jump are very popular, and they have no difficult skills to master, or rules to learn.

What makes your product different? Space Hopper could be the next big game. It combines an element of nostalgia for older iPhone users, but it is very simple and fun, so kids will enjoy it, too.

Name of App Store application you are assessing; Space Hopper
The information below will help you assess your App Store application. By addressing all four areas, you can make your application stronger and more likely to be a success.

Questions to consider

Does your application do something unique?

Is there anything innovative about it?

What are its USPs (unique selling points)?

Why will people use this application instead of a different application?

Strengths

The Space Hopper game has novelty value and will attract older users who remember playing on real Space Hoppers when they were children.

It uses the iPhone's motion sensor to make the Space Hopper bounce; therefore, it is very easy to use for people of all ages.

Why wouldn't people use this application?

Does it do everything it says it can?

Is it as good or better than other similar applications already available?

Do you have a technical support team in place in case people have problems with the application?

Weaknesses

It is a new game from a brand-new developer, so we have to start building users from scratch, against other much more well-established app manufacturers.

If you are shaking your iPhone to make the Space Hopper bounce, it is not always easy to see the phone screen and avoid obstacles.

Can the application be improved in the future, e.g. more features added?

Will new markets emerge for this application?

Can the application target new "niche" (i.e., small, specific) markets?

Can it be used globally?

Can it develop new USPs?

Opportunities

Could look great and be even more fun on an iPad.

Research may show that Space Hoppers were also popular in other countries, therefore increasing the market for the app.

There is no language element to the game, so it can easily be played internationally.

Is the market for applications shrinking?

Will new technology make the application unnecessary?

Are any of the weaknesses so bad that they might affect the application in the long run?

Is Apple likely to decide to remove applications from its site?

Threats

As Space Hoppers are not a new invention, another company may produce a better game using the same idea.

People will get bored playing one single game and will want something new. For the company's continued success, we will need to develop more games.

Do You Have What it Takes to Work at Apple? Try This!

1) When you look at a computer, do you think:
a) Great, what's on YouTube?
b) I wish I had an iMac — in blue to match my bedroom.
c) If the screen was flatter, and the keyboard was built into the hard drive, this would look pretty cool!

2) If you were asked to redesign the iPod, would you say:
a) No chance, just let me listen to it!
b) Well, I'd like a touchscreen that doesn't show fingerprints.
c) Great! I've got 20 ideas already.

3) You're given a pencil and paper, and asked to create something new. Do you:
a) Write your name in bubble writing.
b) Draw your favorite cartoon of Mr. Tomkins, the science teacher.
c) Create a new design for a music player that fits inside wireless headphones.

4) When you buy a pair of speakers, what do you look for?
a) I don't — my mom buys them for me.
b) I like to have what's popular at the time.
c) I spend a lot of time assessing design and performance. They need to look good and feel good.

5) Name one product you would love to own.
a) A never-ending bag of salt and vinegar potato chips.
b) I want a flat-screen TV for my bedroom!
c) The Alessi "Juicy Salif" lemon squeezer would be cool.

6) Who is your favorite designer?
a) Do Nike and Adidas count?
b) After reading this book, it's got to be Jonathan Ive!
c) Ettore Sottsass — he designed everything from typewriters to buildings.

7) Whenever Apple launches a new product, do you think:
a) Have they launched a cheaper iPod yet?
b) Excellent — something for my Christmas list!
c) I'd love to get behind the scenes and see the thought processes that went in to making that.

Results

Mostly As: Sorry, but your chances of working at Apple are looking shaky! It doesn't sound like you have the interest in design to succeed at this world-famous company.

Mostly Bs: You're aware of design, but you need to give it more time and attention if you want to succeed in a design-led business.

Mostly Cs: It sounds like you have what it takes to get a job at Apple! Keep working hard at school, and pushing to be the best, and who knows?

application A computer program designed to help people perform a specific activity, for example, word processing.

arrogant Showing a high opinion of one's own importance and abilities.

axing Closing down; terminating.

binary code A system of numbers, only using 0s and 1s, which gives a computer instructions on what to do.

chaotic Badly organized or confused.

circuit board A piece of material that holds all the electronic parts that go into a computer.

component A part of something, in this case a computer, that goes into making the whole. For example, the screen and the keyboard are components.

corporate culture The way a company is run.

emit To give off or send out.

facilitate To assist the progress of.

high-resolution graphics High-quality images, in this case on a computer. The higher the resolution, the more image detail you see.

hobbyist Someone who pursues something for pleasure.

innovation Something newly introduced, like a new piece of technology or a new way of doing something.

must-have device Something that looks and works so well that everyone wants to own one.

operating system The program that runs your computer and makes it work.

radiation Energy that is transmitted or spread in the form of rays, waves or particles. Ionizing radiation can be dangerous and cause cancer.

retailer A company that sells goods in small quantities to consumers.

revenue A company's income before costs are taken into account; gross income.

scout A person sent out to gain information.

Silicon Valley An area in northern California close to San Francisco that is home to the world's largest technology companies.

spreadsheet A program used in accounting, which can track finances and other data in a table with columns and rows.

tablet PC A flat-screen, handheld PC with a touchscreen keyboard.

techie Someone who has high levels of ability in computer programming.

telecommunications The science of communication through telephones, radio, television and so on.

thrive To do well; prosper.

American Computer Museum
2023 Stadium Drive, Unit 1-A
Bozeman, MT 59715
(406) 582-1288
Web site: http://www.compustory.com
This museum's mission is to collect, preserve, interpret and display the artifacts and history of the information age.

Apple Inc.
1 Infinite Loop
Cupertino, CA 95014
(408) 996-1010
Web site: http://www.apple.com
Apple designs Macs, personal computers, along with OS X, iLife, iWork and professional software. The company leads the digital music revolution with its iPods and iTunes online store. Apple has reinvented the mobile phone with the iPhone and has introduced the iPad mobile media and computing device.

Computer History Museum
1401 N. Shoreline Boulevard
Mountain View, CA 94043
(650) 810-1010
Web site: http://www.computerhistory.org
The Computer History Museum is dedicated to the preservation and celebration of computing history. It is home to one of the largest international collections of computing artifacts in the world, encompassing computer hardware, ephemera, photographs, moving images, documents and software.

IT History Society
One Blackfield Drive, Suite 331
Tiburon, CA 94920
Web site: http://www.ithistory.org
This organization's mission is to enhance and expand works concerning the history of information technology and to demonstrate the value of IT history to the understanding and improvement of our present and future world.

New Mexico Museum of Natural History and Science
1801 Mountain Road NW
Albuquerque, NM 87104
(505) 841-2800
Web site: http://www.nmnaturalhistory.org
This museum features a permanent exhibition dedicated to the history of the microcomputer, the machine that revolutionized the way we live, work and play. Called STARTUP, the gallery features one-of-a-kind artifacts, video and interactive displays.

The Tech Museum
201 South Market Street
San Jose, CA 95113
Web site: http://www.thetech.org
The museum's Silicon Valley Innovation Gallery showcases the amazing range of Silicon Valley technological innovation and creativity.

Web Sites

Due to the changing nature of Internet links, Rosen Publishing has developed an online list of Web sites related to the subject of this book. This site is updated regularly. Please use this link to access the list:

http://www.rosenlinks.com/bht/app